"It's how you pick the crab"

An Oral Portrait of Eastern Shore Crab Picking

by Kelly Feltault and the
Crab Pickers of the Eastern Shore

CHESAPEAKE BAY MARITIME MUSEUM · THE BREENE M. KERR CENTER FOR CHESAPEAKE STUDIES

CONTENTS

(above) Crab pickers working at Samuel S. Coston Crab Company, Hampton, Virginia, circa 1910. *Photo: Blue Ridge Heritage Archive.*

(right) Seafood Buyer 1:4, 1938. *Gardner Lamson Collection, Chesapeake Bay Maritime Museum.*

OLDEST CRABMEAT PACKERS IN THE
WORLD

ESTABLISHED 1878

McMENAMIN & CO., Inc.

Floyd W. Moore, Manager

PACKERS OF

FRESH CRABMEAT AND HARD CRABS

LARGE DeLUXE LUMPS

HAMPTON,   VIRGINIA

For those who live on the Chesapeake Bay, spring brings the anticipation of warmer weather and the year's first crab cakes—a hunger for the essence of summer. The Atlantic blue crab became more than a local Chesapeake delicacy in 1878 when McMenamin and Company in Hampton, Virginia, perfected the process of canning fresh picked crabmeat, shipping it by steamboat to Baltimore and by train across the nation. They began a nationwide demand for Chesapeake crab and factories opened around the Bay, employing hundreds of women to pick crabmeat by hand. By the 1930s the industry supported over 150 crab houses, and the number continued to rise after World War II. The industry reached its zenith in 1949 when Maryland packing houses could not keep up with the volume of crabs brought in by watermen. Early in the season, packers limited their daily purchase to one thousand pounds of crabs per day, but by the fall they stopped buying crabs entirely.

The blue crab made Eastern Shore towns such as Crisfield, St. Michaels, and Cambridge famous for their crabmeat brands. But behind the famous labels worked a predominantly female labor force. Picking houses relied on the traditional skills of local women who needed to earn a living to support their families by working ten to twelve hour shifts for thirty-five cents a gallon throughout the 1930s and '40s. These workers produced one of the first seafood worker's unions in the nation and a unique women's culture built around their world of work.

Today the wages are higher, but the crabs are fewer and smaller. A declining annual crab harvest and competition from foreign crab imports closed a majority of packing houses by the end of the twentieth century. Now as you drive into Crisfield, once known as the "Seafood Capital of the Nation," the beautiful swimmer of the Chesapeake Bay catches your eye, but not in the watermen's bushels or on the docks. Instead, the red figure of the blue crab graces the street signs, billboards, and the town water tower soaring overhead. The echo of earlier prosperity also lingers in the memories and skills of the people who earned a living in the Bay's crab factories.

The Chesapeake Bay Maritime Museum set out to record these memories from the remaining generations of the Bay's crab factory workers. These workers also explained the challenges facing the industry at a time when many people foresee its demise. What follows is more than the history of the industry, it is the story of the industry's place in the lives of the workers. This is an oral portrait of the Eastern Shore's crab pickers and of an industry that shaped not only their lives, but also much of our own ideas of summer.

Photo: Kelly Feltault.

Yesterday's Crab House

Unloading crabs at Meredith and Meredith Inc.
Photo: Kelly Feltault.

*M*odern crab houses do not need to be on the shoreline. Built of cinderblock and cement, they operate with electricity, refrigeration, and trucks. Their interiors gleam from stainless steel tables and countertops. But these are the constructions of modern health regulations, and not the crab houses older pickers remember. Their factories were built of wood and crowded the shorelines, or sat perched atop pilings in the channels of the Chesapeake.

My father worked at Charles Parks when I was a child back in the '20s and '30s—they're still in crab picking even today. And my mother picked crabs there, Mrs. Parks taught her. This factory was where the steamboats came and it had a freight office attached, so it was quite an active center for freight and passengers going to Baltimore.

The floor was wooden in the factory; there was no cement floor like today. At one time, my mother and father lived right there. They had an apartment above the crab house, which was way out in the water on the long wooden wharf. I would think because of the steamboat, it had to be out in the channel. And I learned to count to a hundred there, to count peeler crabs from the crabbers bringing them in.

—Evelyn Robinson, crab picker

Watermen sold their crabs directly to the picking houses, pulling up alongside the factory's docks to unload their barrels of crabs. From the docks, crabs passed to the workers' hands following a sequential process divided by gender and pay.

First, men steamed the crabs. From here, they shoveled them onto the picking tables for the women to extract the meat. The crab pickers brought their meat to a counter where it was weighed and packed for shipping—the final step for a gallon of crabmeat until it reached a consumer in New York or as far west as Colorado and Texas

STEAMING

When I first got into the business, we had just the upright boiler that used soft coal. You had to make the fire up with the kindling and then it took a while to get the steam up—and you kept it up all day. We had one man who tended the boiler; that was his job. But then, in later years, we got into the oil-fired boilers, they were all automatic—you just flip the switch and it comes on. Then we had the round cookers that held fifteen barrels, which is about sixteen, seventeen hundred pounds of crabs in each one. It was a roll-type thing using live steam. It was a stainless steel cooker that was round and had a perforated steam pipe that went through it, and when they turned the steam on, all that steam would come out of these perforated pipes and steam the crabs. Well, you put a top on it and you fastened it down as tight as you could, but still steam escaped from it and that's the way we did it for many years.

—*Roy Harrison*, manager, Harrison and Jarboe Seafood

I guess the best time, really, us kids used to have is when the steamer used to blow out, and we'd pick up all the crabs. The top of the steamer would blow off, blow all the way across on the other side of the plant where the oyster shell mill was.

—*Donald Cephas*, claw cracker

Yeah, I remember that. We would have to run and get out of the crab house. All this steam would come out from too much pressure; steam be everywhere!

—*Rosalie Brown*, crab picker

Roll-steamer for crabs, Rock Point, Maryland, 1941. Photo: Reginald Hotchkiss, U. S. Department of Agriculture, FSA. Library of Congress.

Well, we all helped to design the steaming operation, because when I first came in the industry, they were cooked in big wooden boxes. Big large cookers, several hundred pounds, and they rolled over and dumped 'em onto the floor. And of course, they were not steamed under pressure. So we wound up as part of the industry changes by cooking crabs under pressure, but we didn't get electricity down here until the late '40s. So we had a little 110-volt generator, and we worked on a 32-volt battery system for lights and so forth.

—*Calvert Tolley*, retired owner, Meredith and Meredith Inc.

PICKING

Priscilla Tolley at work at Meredith and Meredith Inc.
Photo: Kelly Feltault.

The watermen sold their crabs to the packer and most of times their wives and all would go to that same factory and pick. My husband sold his crabs over to W.T. Ruark's where his mom picked, and that's the reason I mainly picked there.

—*Nellie Flowers,* crab picker

It was crabs upon crabs caught then. You went to work early because we did not have coolers—they were spread out to cool, and you shoveled them off the floor. They dumped the steam boxes and spread them out probably about a foot thick that night as they steamed them. And when you'd go over in the morning, you'd look to see how many crabs you had to pick that day. And you had to pick all that you had because you did not have a cooler to put them in. That was only in later years that I saw crabs put in a cooler.

—*Evelyn Robinson,* crab picker

When I first started picking back in the Depression, we used what they call Barlow knives, and then they were outlawed. They had a wooden handle, and they were outlawed on account of bacteria in the wood. Then we used a solid stainless steel knife that had no cracks or anything so it wouldn't build up any bacteria.

—*Lib Dunleavy,* crab picker

Back then you picked in pans. See that's been a many year ago. Two pans—one pan for backfin, and one for your regular. That's what you called it then. Back then we had two grades of meat—backfin and regular. And now it's graded a little different because we have the jumbo lump.

—*Nicey Turpin,* crab picker and shop steward

We had bushel baskets to put the crab trash in, not like today, we have trash barrels. And you turned one basket over, and you put the other basket on it. And they didn't wash the wooden floor down every night; they put lime on it. At the end of the week, they would wash it all down good, but they would lime it down. And we didn't have stainless steel tables in there. They were all wooden, like a big bend all the way around. We called it the bend; it ran all the way across the building. And that's what the people called it, "Put me some crabs in my bend."

—*Laurena Collemer,* crab picker

PACKING AND SHIPPING

Most of the equipment, or a lot of the equipment, that is used comes from tomato canning factories. Tomato canning was around before crabs, so they just borrowed some of the equipment—the crab cooker, the retort, and the canning machines for sealing metal cans for pasteurizing—were all from tomato canning factories.

—Tim Howard,
 owner and manager,
 Maryland Crab Meat Company

We have canning equipment here from the old Continental Can Company that's dated 1906. And they're still in working condition—very few parts left for 'em though. If you need parts for 'em they have to be custom made, and I go to the machine shop to make 'em. They still work fine. I mean they seal just as well as any new machine. In fact, they claim that they're better than the new machines. I haven't seen a new machine, ever.

—Jim Dodson,
 owner and manager,
 Byrd's Seafood

Crab cookers like these are still in use around the Bay.
Photo: A. Aubrey Bodine Collection, The Mariner's Museum, Newport News, Va.

Picking houses had huge iceboxes, icehouses they called them, that the walls were insulated with sawdust. They got these big cakes of ice, like hundred-pound cake of ice and they had this grinder that you'd put it in to grind up the ice. The ice was put in these big wooden barrels that you would pack your crabmeat in, and you put this cover over it with a wooden rim around it, and that's how you shipped it. Each barrel would be your regular crabmeat or special. Or maybe if that person ordered a mix—if he wanted twenty-five pounds of each, you put it in these barrels and then you put a tag on it with his name and his address. And it was shipped by steamboat.

—Evelyn Robinson, crab picker

Crabmeat packed in barrels, ready for shipping from J. M. Clayton Company dock, circa 1940s.
Photo: Joyce Jones.

After World War II, when I started out, we didn't have a cooler; we didn't have refrigeration. We carried products to the local ice plant, right down the street here, where we bought ice. They delivered it by truck, chopped up in a bag. Back then we put all the product in a twenty-gallon barrel, everything went in a great big barrel. They had different sizes; you had a ten-gallon barrel, a five-gallon barrel, twelve-gallon barrel. Twenty-gallon barrel was the largest. That weighed about two hundred and fifty pounds after you got through packing it with crabmeat.There was not any boxes like we have today.

—*I.T. Todd*, owner, Metompkin Seafood

Byrd's was an old company here from, I guess, in the '50s. Clifford Byrd is the one that started the pasteurization of the crabmeat. He didn't even want to get into the crab picking industry He just wanted to have this process of how to preserve crabmeat. You know, when there was an abundance of it, he could can it, and then it could be used later. And it's the same process that is used in the industry today. He figured it out and had a patent on it until 1976. He did all the pasteurization of the crabmeat in Crisfield for all the packing houses here years ago back in the '50s and '60s. He would pasteurize it and then send it back to them.

—*Jim Dodson*, owner and manager, Byrd's Seafood

Regulations first began to affect the production process in the early 1900s during an outbreak of typhoid from Chesapeake seafood. The Virginia Dairy and Food Division reported crab picking factories in Hampton converted to metal covered tables and stainless steel knives as early as 1911 while Maryland required stainless steel equipment by law in 1957.

The most difficult thing about running this plant back then was the Health Department. I mean to keep everything clean. We were the first ones, I guess, in the area that got a boiler big enough to operate a steam cleaner. It's a high-pressure hose, and you mix water and steam and the pressure increases as you're mixing it. And that does a real good job in cleaning your equipment, your tables, your floors, your walls—it cuts paint right off the wall.

—*J. Clayton Brooks*, retired owner, J. M. Clayton Company

Electricity really changed the way we operated our picking houses quite a bit. We were able to do some more things sanitary wise—keep the product better, install refrigeration, making our own ice and all that sort of thing. It ran pumps to do wash downs of the factory and all this sort of thing. Of course, we had pumps before, but they were gasoline motors.

—*Calvert Tolley*, retired owner, Meredith and Meredith Inc.

Memories of a Life Spent Picking: Childhood

Maryland's child labor laws of 1894, which made it illegal to employ children under the age of twelve in factories, specifically exempted the canning industry and eight counties of the Eastern Shore. This continued until 1912 when it became unlawful to employ children under the age of twelve in any canning factory. Six years later, the state raised the age to fourteen and required a signed "evidence of age certificate" and a completed physical. Meanwhile, federal laws continued to exempt the seafood industry.

Despite these state regulations, children continued to work in canning factories. Crab pickers were paid by the pounds they picked, known as the piece rate system, and families relied on the children to supplement the family income. Parents added their children's pounds of picked crabmeat to their own gallon cans for a daily total. Even the children of factory owners found themselves working in the family business.

Picking crabs was a family thing. All the people that worked here when I started around age seven was family—and that was over fifty years ago. Most of 'em had about six, seven to twelve kids, and everybody worked together.

When we was coming up, people would say, "I thought it's about time they brought you down here." Because they know that if anyone has a child, they're looking for them to come down here after they got a certain age. And that's the way they would take care of the baby-sitters and all the rest. Most of the parents bring 'em down here, then after they got down here they said, "Well, you're going to do something." And, of course, a lot of us didn't like it.

—*Donald Cephas,* claw cracker

We didn't have babysitters back then on Hooper's Island, so mama would take us to the crab house—some people even brought their playpens in there. There wasn't any law then that you couldn't keep the children out of the crab house—and even after there was, I still brought my own kids down. We thought we were having a good time because we didn't know any different, you know. It was just the way that everybody lived.

—*Laurena Collemer,* crab picker

I learned to pick from my mother-in-law after I was married. Up to then I had worked in a tomato canning factory. I started out cracking claws even though I was twenty-one; you always start out cracking claws at first. And then my sister and I just decided we were going to start picking crabs because they would leave us in the factory with all the claws. Of course in them days we had to crack all the claws, no matter how small they were.

—*Nellie Flowers*, crab picker

Well it was a pain with the kids running around. Of course, the mothers tried to teach the kids how to crack the claws, but they couldn't always do it. And it was like a nursery around here. Of course they learn how to pick crabs from their mother, they picked right alongside their mother or in a table so the mother could watch 'em. And that's how our future crab pickers would develop. The mother would teach 'em, and she had 'em right there with her.

—*J. Clayton Brooks*, retired owner, J. M. Clayton Company

I hated it. I wanted to do anything other than this. When I was a kid, I would work every summer doing all those little things that no one else wanted to do. All the cans for the day had to be dipped in a sanitizer. So I'd be given a stack of a thousand cans and had to dip every one of them. Turn them upside down; count them out in lots of a hundred, made sure everyone had ice in their bin, made sure everyone had paper towels, and carrying the meat up and bringing it back to the pickers—things like that. And I did that every summer, for years. It was always my summer job.

—*Tim Howard*, owner and manager, Maryland Crab Meat Company.

My mother Fronie Jones started with J.M. Clayton Company on Hooper's Island originally. She started at eight years old standing on a box picking crabs. Then she would go to school and come back to the factory after school and work. When the company moved to Cambridge in 1920 she followed the company there and she married my father who also worked here. He bought a house, and she picked crabs. That was all I think she could do at that time. So she stayed here at Clayton's picking crabs eighty some years before she died.

I started cracking claws when I was twelve years old; my mother brought me in. And I worked in the morning then went to school and came back in the afternoon and finished like she had. I worked here until I was twenty and then moved away, but I came back after mom died, started working back here about five years ago.

—*Rosalie Brown*, crab picker

EVADING THE LAW

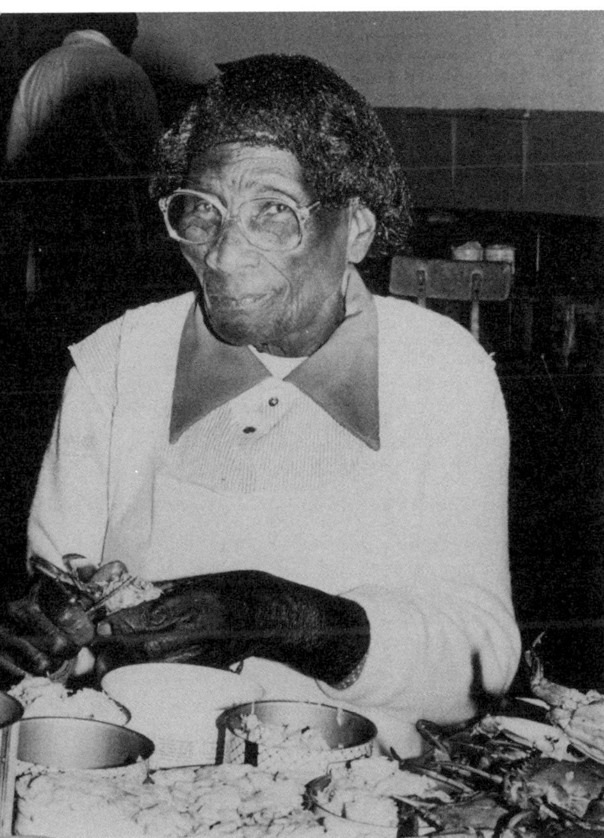

Fronie Jones working at J. M. Clayton Company.
Photo: Rosalie Brown.

You wouldn't know the inspectors were coming—they didn't give you any advance notice. But they'd always hit like in the front of the building first. Well, then it went through the building like wildfire, you know. One person would say, "We've got inspectors." And it would go down, just keep going from table to table. And all over the factory, everybody knew they were there.

—Lib Dunleavy, crab picker

If the inspector or somebody came, mom would either make us go out of the crab house, or I can remember at that time they had big cans, big trash cans that they picked in. And if some of 'em were empty or something, they would probably tell you get down in that can. And you sit down in that can; it was fun then 'cause you were hiding.

—Joyce Fitchett, champion crab picker

I think I was about thirteen when they really got strict, and I had to leave Clayton Company here in Cambridge. I went down the county to another crab house where the inspector didn't want to make that trip down there. And then at fourteen, I came back here because you just needed a doctor's certificate to work and they had a company doctor. They might take your pressure or something like that and then say, "Okay, you all right to work."

—Donald Cephas, claw cracker

LEARNING RESPONSIBILITY

Laurena Collemer picking crabs. *Photo: Kelly Feltault.*

I was the youngest in my family, and I picked crabs like the rest of my family, but I didn't shuck oysters. My sisters did, but they never graduated high school. They had to work and help. Mama bought a house when we were growing up, and I was nine years old when we moved to the new house. But they all worked to help mom to pay for the house.

It had rooms that we never even had furnished. But we worked, and my two sisters bought a living room suit, paid so much on it a week. And then I bought an Oriental rug. It was beautiful, it was just one of those beautiful wine-colored rugs, you know. And we had that on the floor, and we were growing up, learning responsibility.

—*Laurena Collemer*, crab picker

I cracked claws at Tilghman Packing Company as a teenager after working at Harrison and Jarboe. And with some of that money I bought my school clothes at Miss Grace; she would get all the latest fashions from New York. My mother didn't mind as long as I used the money to buy my clothes. I had to give my mother, I think it was about ten or five dollars a week for food when I first started working. But that had to come out of my money before I spent anything on the clothes. But if I decided that I was not going to save out my five or ten dollars, then I had to eat with my grandmother or somewhere the next week because I didn't eat at home.

—*Alice Palmer*, crab picker

Basically, I've worked most of my life. Started young and I'm still going, thank God. It's made me realize that you got to work for what you want and I do that. I do what I have to do. And I have at times worked three jobs just to survive. I've worked the restaurants, maybe a half a day, and I'd work housecleaning for somebody and I pick a few crabs here and there. It's just helped me to know that in order to get anything in life, you have to work for it.

—*Joyce Fitchett*, champion crab picker

You have to look at it from their point of view, from the parents' point of view. What you made as a child was pretty good money. When you say fifty dollars, don't sound like very much, but you talk about fifty or seventy years ago, fifty dollars was a lot of money. And most people didn't work down here to have big homes and such. I got fifty cents a week in the summer time, and one week I made forty dollars. I couldn't figure why I only got fifty cents out of it. Do you see what I'm saying?

And there would be families down here in the course of a day would only have one number to weigh your meat towards, and they were putting on that number two hundred to three hundred pounds per day because the kids' totals went on that number.

—*Donald Cephas*, claw cracker

"AN HONEST DAY'S WORK"

Crab pickers often make two remarks about their work—"crab picking is an honest day's work" and factories were "like one big family." Their memories of those days of work include juggling family responsibilities with long hours. Individual experiences differ according to race and age, and many recall working in racially mixed picking rooms as early as the 1920s. All are still proud to call themselves crab pickers and their "own boss."

At one point we operated several plants, one in St. Michaels and another on Hooper's Island. It was strange the way the pickers would work at several plants on the island. They would go to work at our plant at twelve o'clock at night and they'd work 'till seven in the morning. Then the plant would close until twelve the next night. Those same pickers would go on to another plant and work after ours closed. They must have worked all of the time almost down there.

—*Roy Harrison*, manager, Harrison and Jarboe Seafood

You'd have to take care of your home, and your washing, and your ironing and everything just the same as any other individual would keep a house. But you learned to do it around your work. I was very fortunate because a lot of the time, my mother was living with me and she would have my dinner ready in the evening when I came home.

—*Lib Dunleavy*, crab picker

Leona Spicer picking crabs at Meredith and Meredith Inc.
Photo: Kelly Feltault.

Fronie Jones and Georgia Cephas picking crabs. *Photo: Richard Dodds.*

I'll tell you something about the dignity of it. I was a lab technician before I moved to Smith Island. And when I moved over here, people would say, "Well, Christine, what are you going to do now?" and I said pick crabs. And they sort of frowned on it. And I'm just as proud right now of my work as anybody else is because it's an honest living. It's the only thing that I can do to make a living here, and I'm proud of my product and what we do. Like when you hear people say, "God, she picks crabs for a living. Is that the only job she's got?" Like I said, it's hard work, and you've got to dig your heels in when you're going to do it, you can't fool around with it. You've got to stick to it every day and get 'em picked off, but it's a good, decent way to make a living and to help your family and your husband pay the bills.

—*Christine Smith,* crab picker, Smith Island Crab Meat Co-Operative

Well my mother, Fronie Jones, always said a hard day's work wouldn't hurt anybody. And she was a hard-working lady.

—*Nicie Jones*

Oh, She would work all day, go home, fix something to eat, and come back and work all night. I couldn't do it. I'm not telling a story. I couldn't do it.

—*Georgia Cephas*

I recall one time I tried that schedule with her. We were sitting there picking crabs and I was sitting with my back hunched over. She says, "Baby, what's a matter?" I said, "Grandmom, my back hurt." "Oh, my Lord, child, you ain't got no back," she tells me. I told her, "Look, I'm not made of the same thing you made out of, so my back is hurting." When we got off, I went home, fell across my bed—smelly crab clothes and all. And Grandma went home, fixed something to eat, cleaned up her house, took her bath and went shopping. I was still asleep across my bed.

— *Joyce Jones*

— *Nicie Jones, Georgia Cephas, and Joyce Jones,* relatives of Fronie Jones, three generations of crab pickers.

The Depression forced many Americans to migrate to other areas in search of work. The Eastern Shore was no exception, and families moved from one seafood town to another, often seasonally. Throughout the 1930s and '40s, African American workers and white women sought out one of the few jobs open to them—crab picking. These migrations created inter-racial picking rooms, some of which were integrated, but this did not extend beyond the workplace. Crab pickers went home to segregated communities.

> The Easton plant had the shanties back in the '30s and a lot of these people would live there the year around. They'd work in tomatoes, of course the company insisted they work in tomatoes when they were running, and then when the tomato season was over they would come down and shuck oysters, pick crabs, shuck clams or whatever. And they'd live right on the camp year around. They were nothing but shanties.
>
> —*Roy Harrison*, manager,
>   Harrison and Jarboe Seafood

> My family's originally from Norfolk, Virginia, and around Cape Charles, Virginia. Well it seems like work was scarce where we were, and my uncle decided that he would move the family. He moved the family to St. Michaels because of the seafood factories.
>
> —*Alice Palmer*, claw cracker and crab picker

SEGREGATION

When I was young we had mixed crab houses around Hooper's Island, black people and white people, down on the island. Then we went to all white crab houses. I think what happened was most of the black people moved away or died, the older people did. And the young people did not want to pick crabs. You went through a period when we were all white crab houses. And now, when I went back to picking, black people had returned to the crab houses around Hoopersville.

—*Evelyn Robinson*, crab picker

At the Cambridge plant we had, that was in 1940, they were one-third white and two-thirds black. And the whites set to themselves and the blacks too, which was normal because they had their own thing going I guess. They wanted to talk about the things they talked about. They talked all day long.

—*Roy Harrison*, manager, Harrison and Jarboe Seafood

Things were segregated but the picking room was joined together. They just had an imaginary partition, imaginary that you know which way not to go. Then you could sit anywheres. I thought about that a long time ago. Although it was segregated at that time, down here we were the majority as far as working in the plant. That's the only time we ever got-over during that time.

You see, as far as carrying the crabs out, of course we been doing that for years. But if the crab carrier will carry out the best crabs in that white area, and the black crab pickers would see something like that, then all they have to do is raise their voice about it and it would not be done no more. You understand what I mean now? There wouldn't been no crab house here without those black women, they was tough women.

—*Donald Cephas*, claw cracker

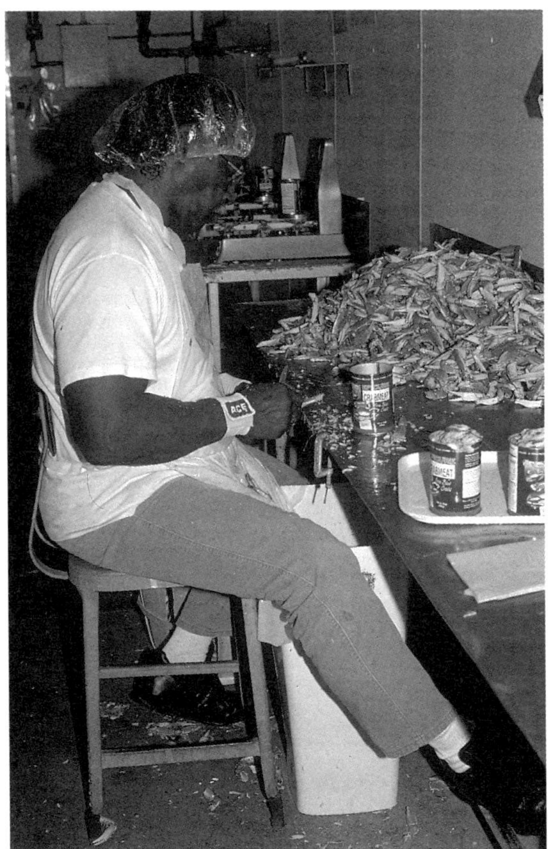

Donald Cephas cracking claws. *Photo: Kelly Feltault.*

They integrated high schools here when I was in the tenth grade, and I met this girl in high school, Edith, and I knew her because I'd grown up with her. I literally grew up with her ever day of the summer, and then all of a sudden we were thrown together in the tenth grade, but I knew these people here at the factory. I grew up knowing "Pete," here. When we went to school, I met this girl and they were calling her "Edith" and I didn't know who Edith was and I called her Pete. And all the black kids that knew her were amazed—here was a white kid calling their friend Pete because no one knew her as Pete other than the blacks.

—*Tim Howard,* owner and manager, Maryland Crab Meat Company

In the '80s I was down on Hooper's Island cracking some claws. And they had the same old sign that they had a thousand years ago in the sense—they didn't have the name up there 'white' and 'coloreds' bathroom—but you know which one to go into. So when the boss man said to me, "You know, we're just like one big happy family down here." I said, "Is that right?" I said, "My family house, we all use the same bathroom." He didn't say no more about that from that point on. When you talked to him, you talk about work. Don't tell me about no happy family. I knew it was no happy family.

—*Donald Cephas,* claw cracker

Most everybody worked in the factories, like shucking oysters and skinning tomatoes and picking crabs in St. Michaels. And the younger ones went to college and became teachers, doctors, and different things. But seafood money got them there.

—*Alice Palmer,* claw cracker and crab picker

WAGES, LABOR, AND UNIONS

The rise of the crab picking industry in the 1930s coincided with the emergence of the modern labor movement. A volatile time for many industries in America, the unionism of Eastern Shore crab pickers was no exception as it mirrored national conflicts related to wages around the country.

Packing house owners were predominantly white with a few exceptions such as African American owned Coulbourne and Jewett Seafood, Turner Seafood, and Jones Sanitary Seafood Company. In Crisfield and Hampton, crab pickers were predominantly African American while north of Crisfield crab factories employed white and black crab pickers.

Men in the factories received an hourly wage. Crab pickers and claw crackers, usually women, were paid "by the piece," or by how many pounds they picked. They received no insurance or benefits. Piece rates changed based on the demand or availability of the crabs. Packing house owners stood placards in front of their factories to notify pickers of changing rates. Pickers were free to work at any crab house paying a higher wage, but often packing houses throughout a city would lower their rates simultaneously.

> Well I think the first time I ever picked crabs was in about—it must've been '31 or '32. It was during the Depression. And they often laugh around here when I tell them that we picked crabs for three cents a pound at that time. And the youngsters around here, they can't realize that.
>
> —*Lib Dunleavy,* crab picker

My land, let's see. We got paid by the pound. Over there in Talbot I don't think it was hardly a dollar a gallon. Not too much. Here in Crisfield they used to get more than they did over in Talbot County. But it would be five pounds, five pounds a dollar. That's what it was. Dollar a gallon.

> —*Nicey Turpin,*
> crab picker and shop steward

These were desperate times in the packing business right before World War II and a lot of them really had no capital because of the Depression. After the war, there were about fifteen to seventeen crab picking plants in Crisfield, some of them quite sizeable. This was really the high point of the crab picking business in town. They made a lot of money during World War II because you had food rationing during the war but seafood was not rationed. And the prices went up and, of course, it made quite a difference.

> —*I.T. Todd,* owner, Metompkin Seafood

These people never made a lot of money, and I kept trying to get all the plants to raise the price of the picking. We couldn't raise it unless other plants raised because we wouldn't be competitive. And I felt sorry for the pickers because they worked hard and they didn't make a lot of money. They should have been making a lot more.

We did go up later, maybe a few cents a pound above the rest. I think eventually the others had to do it because they were losing pickers by not doing it. Fact is we sent a bus to Cambridge. We needed pickers anyway, and we sent the bus over there to pick up some of the pickers and offer them more money. Well that got Clayton Company and Todd Company all upset and I think we edged it up a few pennies that way.

—*Roy Harrison,* manager, Harrison and Jarboe Seafood

The conditions in packing houses were appalling during the '30s and '40s. Actually, some of the people were not even getting paid for what they did; packers would take their measurement of a gallon to their own discretion. In other words, what I think is a gallon is not what really is a gallon. Some of the places had no heat in the winter and no coolness in the summer, and they worked under what you might call the worst conditions. And back then, they didn't have anything like OSHA; lots of the buildings were even unsafe.

—*Orlando Purnell,* last President of Local 453

A compromise was reached in the 1931 strike between the pickers and packers, only to see the packers disregard it in the end. Strikes continued throughout the 1930s until the newly formed National Labor Relations Board forced packers to obey the new labor laws created by the Wagner Act of 1935. Crab pickers from Crisfield, Maryland, eventually started one of the first seafood worker's unions in the United States under the Congress of Industrial Organization's [CIO] United Cannery, Agricultural, Packing and Allied Workers of America [UCAPAWA]. UCAPAWA represented black and Hispanic women cannery workers in California and sought out cannery workers on the East Coast. The crab pickers later switched to an AFL affiliate in the 1940s with Albert Bell as the union president. Seafood workers continued to strike throughout the 1950s as far north as Hooper's Island.

Organizers Car Overturned and Burned

"Crisfield was quiet but tense today following a night which brought clashes with union organizers attempting to bring the town's crab pickers into the CIO ranks.

It was the first violence of the three-week old strike in which persons employed to pick crabmeat at seafood plants here are protesting a wage cut.

The calm of the wage dispute between the pickers—mostly women, many of them negroes—and the seafood packing plants was broken for the first time last night when a group of men gathered at a negro settlement here. . .The men, failing to find the organizers, seized their automobile and burned it."

—*Salisbury Times,*
April 22, 1938.

Postcard from McKinley Jones to President Roosevelt requesting a union in Crisfield, March 24, 1940. *Photo: Federal Mediation and Conciliation Service, National Archives II.*

We had a person to leave Crisfield and go to Port Norris, New Jersey. His name was McKinley Jones. And he told a gentleman there about the conditions here in Crisfield, and the gentleman asked him would people be willing to join a union and get out of this problem. And he said most certainly so.

The union folks came down for a look-see, as a matter of fact, they came sort of incognito because they knew the problems that people had when you mentioned union people. The point was to get their foot in the door first. And then you can say that I represent the union.

Well, they came here and asked around, and I think one man stood out and that was Mr. Albert Bell. And it sort of evolved from there. There were cards signed and everything. At first the employers in Crisfield did not even want to recognize the National Labor Relations Board. And they saw that if they didn't comply, they would have to pay a fine. So finally they signed the union contract.

It was done in churches, town halls—matter of fact, before they got a building of their own, they used the Elks home for union meetings. And everybody, including Albert Bell had come up through the ranks. They worked in the seafood houses, and they'd seen what went on. Each crab house had its own steward. She was sort of like the liaison between the packers and the union.

Up until 1980, '79 or '80, it was Local 453. After we merged, we became Local 27 because we merged with the hospital union. They had 500,000; we had 400. When I came into office, we had ten crab houses left in Crisfield. We're down now to three. We had eight oyster houses. We're down now to one, that's Metompkin's. Mrs. Paul's came in here with frozen fish, and when they closed up that finished the union completely here. That was March 1990.

—Orlando Purnell, last President Local 453

They still call me the shop steward, but we don't have a union—not now—we don't work enough to have one. Oh, my, but I was shop steward when I used to work over to the other place before we come to this new factory. Was many a year ago. I can't even figure how many years—40 or 50 some, really.

Way back when they was having union meetings I would go. Everybody was gonna go, but shop steward was supposed to go. They would let you know whether you would get a raise that year or not. Albert Bell, and Melvin Tyler, they were the heads of the union. But all those old souls are dead now.

—Nicey Turpin, crab picker and shop steward

Crab pickers had always worked on the piece work system. Even after the Fair Labor and Standards Act of 1938 created a minimum wage system, crab pickers were excluded by regulations at the federal level. The seafood industry remained exempt from the minimum wage law until 1961 when an amendment forced packing house owners to pay crab pickers a minimum wage regardless of how much meat they picked.

We generally started at seven in the morning and worked until they got tired. That's the way it worked in those days, they didn't have any certain hours. They're sort of free-lance; they come in and work when they want to work and they stop when they want and so forth. They knew the hours the plant would be open—unless we ran out of crabs. We ran out of crabs then they went home.

There was a wage and hour law, but seafood didn't come under that for a long time. It was in other businesses, it got in the canning business first I think, before we got into it. Finally they put seafood into it. They had to. When the wage and hour law came in you had to keep their time—when they came in, when they left—that was a job. We didn't use time cards, we'd just put down on their tab sheet where they picked that day, what hours they came in, when they left, and how much they picked. And that was a job trying to keep up with that.

And then a lot of them couldn't make the minimum. We paid by the pound and they had to pick enough to make up whatever the minimum wage was at that time. If they couldn't pick that much, then we had to make up the difference, and that got a little expensive too.

But then the government came along and let us average it up and they'd give an exemption for whatever pickers couldn't make the minimum. We would average it up over the week and we'd apply for an exemption for so much an hour. Say if the wage was two dollars an hour, maybe they couldn't make over a dollar and a quarter an hour picking then they would let us pay her a dollar and a quarter an hour without having to make up anything. Otherwise we'd have had to let them go because a lot of them couldn't even make half of minimum wage. And we just couldn't have done that; we were already short on pickers.

—*Roy Harrison*, manager,
  Harrison and Jarboe Seafood

"Removal of the present exemption will immediately eliminate a large portion of the workers. We refer to those who are either slower or older, and are known as the slow group, and make up 57% of all workers."

Results of the present season have shown that the above was an understatement rather than an overstatement. In fact, had it not been for the cooperation of the Department of Labor in granting temporary 'handicapped' workers permits to about half of the working force, large numbers of packers would have been forced to close their doors. Even so, it was necessary to tell hundreds of workers not even to apply for work because they were too slow. Yet many of these older, slower, workers desperately needed the income they could earn to buy food, and the packers needed their services to keep up their volume of production.

—Statement submitted by *Chesapeake Seafood Packers Association*
  to Special Subcommittee Hearing on Labor, February 16, 1962.

LOST ARTS:
SINGING

Crab houses rang with the sounds of breaking shells, knives banging against metal, and the sound of women talking. The sound that most passersby and plant owners remember though is music, specifically song. Today only two crab houses on the Eastern Shore—Byrd's Seafood in Crisfield, and the Smith Island Crabmeat Co-operative—still sing hymns.

Someone would just start one up and everyone would join in. Was all day you would hear spirituals being sung. And we would sing the old spirituals: *Sweet Our Prayer,* and *Blessed Assurance*, and *My Hope is Built*. And then after we finished one, then someone else maybe over on the other side of the table would get another one going.

It was always something that would be with joy, you know. Very seldom sad, always something with joy, something to keep your motion with picking the crabs. And you get the song, and you get the motion with the picking, and your hands would go fast with your singing, and your movement would make you in rhythm with the song.

When He should come with trumpets sound, oh may I then in Him be found, dressed in his righteousness, alone, thoughtless to stand before the throne. On Christ a solid rock I stand, all other ground is sinking sand, all other ground is sinking sand.

It's three verses to *My Hope is Built*. And mostly, we would grab that chorus and hold onto it for the longest time, we would sing it over, and over, and over. Yes. After you hear the songs, and you get the feel, something within you let you know that it's time for you to either talk or to sing, to express how you feel within yourself. That would build the momentum and then everyone would want to express their self in some way. And what better way to express yourself in a building like that than singing?

The atmosphere of the crab house and all is different from the atmosphere in the church. So why not bring that atmosphere that you had from the church into the crab house and make your job easier for you? Singing the song would bring joy and see, when the joy come, you don't mind what you have to do. And we knew that we had to work, and this was the work that was here for us to do, and so we had to do it.

—*Alice Palmer,* claw cracker and crab picker

Sometimes when they get in here and they have some good crabs to work on, they get to singing right out in the middle of the day, which was an old tradition with the crab house. Like I told you before, they do sing here every morning 9:00. I don't care who's in there, but 9:00 everybody stops and they sing the Lord's prayer here, every morning 9:00.

—*Jim Dodson,* owner, manager, Byrd's Seafood

Oh they loved to sing, yeah. It was beautiful. Mostly toward the end of the day is when they'd start to get tired and then they'd start to sing and, gorgeous. I wish I could have recorded some of that. It was the most beautiful music I ever heard. All kinds of gospel songs. They didn't sing every day, but they would sing several times a week. One would start, and then each one coming in, first thing you know, just about the whole place was singing. And they could really harmonize.

I remember in 1940 when I managed the Cambridge plant we owned, talk about them singing! They came out with a song called *You Are My Sunshine,* you remember that song?

They sang that all day long, that same song. I got so tired—it would sound good, but I mean, I would get tired of listening to that same song. *You Are My Sunshine.* I'll never forget that. Then, in later years, I put in a microphone upstairs so I could talk to them from the office through the speakers downstairs. And I had a thing that you could play music over these speakers. We found that if you played the faster music, they work faster. So we tried to play the faster records—you played the slow records they slowed down. And it helped them; it relaxed them. We played whatever records they requested.

—*Roy Harrison,* manager, Harrison and Jarboe Seafood

You're caught up in the minute of making a living, and you're here with your friends, and things are happening. You sit down and sing a song. You're just sitting there minding your own business just singing away. And then I think one evening we were in here, and a thunderstorm come up real quick. And we get pretty good-size thunderstorms on Smith Island. And a lot of times the men's out on the water, your children are up in Ewell in little skiffs running about, playing ball or something. And some of the women say, "My Lord, I don't know where my youngen is, here it is a coming this storm."

And I don't know who it was started singing a verse of *Till the Storm Passes By.* That was the song we sung. And that become our theme song. Seems like every time a thunderstorm would come up, we'd say let's sing our song. And it was like our little prayer offered up for the Lord to keep our people safe and keep us safe.

—*Janice Marshall,* crab picker
Smith Island Crab Meat Co-Operative

PICKING PRETTY

All professional crab pickers admit that there is an art to picking a crab properly and without any bone—this is when you are picking pretty. This artful skill was taught to children in the picking houses and many admit that it will soon be lost.

> Not so much in the flake or the special meat, but in the way that the lump is picked. By the way the lump is extracted from the crab, the way it's cut, you can look at it and tell that it was done by this lady or another lady. And chances are when their daughter comes in and picks; she's going to do it the same way. And her three daughters and their kids will all do it the same way.
>
> —*Tim Howard,* owner, manager, Maryland Crab Meat Company

> I've never considered myself to be a fast picker; I just picked. And a lady that I worked with right after I graduated high school, Margaret Lee, she was pretty fast so I patterned myself behind her. And it seems as if every time that she would go up with a gallon, I would try to go up with a gallon with her. So eventually, it got so that I picked up my speed and I got faster. After a while, I was beating her—maybe not a whole lot, but two or three pounds maybe. Then it started to be a gallon, two gallons. And in a day, I could come out of there with fifteen, sixteen gallons. The highest I've ever picked was twenty-one gallons—and five pounds equal a gallon.
>
> —*Joyce Fitchett,* champion crab picker

> Coordination's everything in picking a crab. If you don't have coordination, then you can forget it, because really you're not doing very much. And that's why anybody pick crab long enough, if they're any good at it at all, they say they're a professional. I always say that, but it's an art to doing all this. That's why these ladies can talk and not have to look at what they're doing, because they know their hands are working together.
>
> —*Donald Cephas,* claw cracker

Joyce Fitchet with her crab picking trophies.
Photo: Kelly Feltault.

It's not the fastness of it;
it's how you pick the crab.

—*Nellie Flowers,* crab picker

SCENES IN TODAY'S CRAB HOUSE

Today's crab picking plants face global and local challenges that rival ones of earlier years. Labor is still an issue, though now it is a lack of skilled local workers that is one of the main challenges. The other challenge is a shortage of the Atlantic blue crab. Both shortages produced reactions from packers and pickers that have changed the way these family-run crab plants operate and how they view themselves. A few things have not changed. Pickers work on piece rates based on the minimum wage and receive no health insurance. They still extract the meat by hand using stainless steel knives, packing it directly into plastic containers.

SHORTAGE: LABOR

In the 1960s, picking houses began limiting the number of crabs they would purchase because they just did not have the crab pickers to accomplish the job. Crab houses that once employed hundreds in the 1940s found themselves with only a handful of pickers by the early 1970s.

> Some of the younger ones, they got out and got a taste of insurance and retirement benefits. So they started going out and getting jobs elsewhere, and it seemed like to me that was the start of women leaving the island and working in Cambridge. Now in the past, when there was hard times, I remember some of the ladies going to work at Phillips canning factory in Cambridge skinning tomatoes. But it wasn't a permanent thing. When crabs came, they would come back to the crab houses. But it seemed like to me that was the start of the young people leaving and from then on, not too many young people worked in crab houses.
>
> —*Evelyn Robinson, crab picker*

Today you don't have a big labor pool to draw from. I mean there's nobody standing there waiting outside to come in to pick crabs. Anybody that comes in and says I want to pick crabs, all right, come on in. You want 'em to come in and pick crabs. Now years ago, you had that problem. The pickers would lose their seat if they didn't come in. They would lose their seat. Now you cannot have the younger people coming in doing this work. This is why you don't get any experienced crab pickers anymore because they can't come in with their mothers to do it. So now you have to go out and get the foreign labor.

—*Jim Dodson,*
owner and manager,
Byrd's Seafood

"THEY CALL US *JAIBERAS* AT HOME"

—Lily Alarcon, crab picker

Mexican crab pickers at A. E. Phillips Seafood
Photo: Kelly Feltault.

Today when you enter a crab factory you no longer find one hundred African American and white women picking in a large room. Instead you notice a single table with three to five local women picking crabs among twenty to fifty Mexican women. The talk and stories, so prevalent in local picker's memories, are now in Spanish.

One day in 1990, I came to the plant and I had about two hundred bushels of crabs to pick. And I had only three pickers. I just couldn't take it. We needed the crabmeat to fill orders, and we had the crabs. That's not the way to do business. We tried hiring people from Washington D.C. and interviewed probably 100 people, and one actually showed up to work. So I took the step of checking into migrant labor through the federal H2B program, filled out the paperwork and got approved.

It was a nightmare that first summer. The real problem was that they were new workers. This nice little quiet town on the island, bringing all this foreign labor in here that didn't know how to pick. Watermen were fussing. Crab pickers were fussing. Other packers said they'd close up first. Said, "I'll put a lock on the damn door before I hire them." It was just a nightmare. They all got Mexican workers now though. It's over two hundred here on the island now.

—Jay Newcomb, manager, A. E. Phillips Seafood

Guadelupe Garcia Ortiz at work. *Photo: Kelly Feltault.*

Where my sisters and I live in Mexico is a big city—an industrial city. We have a university, big clinics and buildings, but there are not too many opportunities for work. Here we have an opportunity to earn more money. If I work very hard here, what I would make in Mexico working for one whole month, I can earn it here in one week—and I spend less here. Yes, everything is worthwhile—the effort, the sacrifice, the pain involved in the work we do. That is why we keep coming back, because there is an advantage for us in this work and that is why we leave our families behind to work here from April through November.

— *Guadalupe Garcia Ortiz*, crab picker

Most of the Mexican women picking crabs around the Bay come from San Luis Potosi and Hidalgo. They are secretaries, mothers, and even doctors back in Mexico, but seven months of picking crabs pays more than their professions at home.

We cannot save a great amount for ourselves because we are constantly sending money to Mexico. We have a responsibility towards our parents, towards our children, so we constantly send them money. That way I am sure that my family is not suffering, that they have food to put on the table, the necessary medicines if they get sick, enough money to pay the electricity bill on time.

—*Soledad Perez Bernal*, crab picker

In the state of Mayari where I'm from, there is an agent who works with these plants, a recruiter. In the past, he used to hire only men to work in tobacco plantations in Virginia and then he started asking for girls. We did not know why he was suddenly asking for girls and everybody thought he wanted to hire girls to serve as prostitutes. I am not a young woman, so I did not think he would hire me for that. He kept talking about crabs and we did not know what he meant by that.

Each of us decided to take a chance and more than 80 girls came the first year—two busloads. There had never been a girl from Mayari working here, so my daughter and I stayed in North Carolina the first two years. Later, after hearing the other girls talk about this region, I came to work here. The only difference is that here we get paid more. For instance, here if I make forty pounds I get $80.00. In North Carolina, I used to be paid $1.75 per pound of lump meat and $1.45 per pound of small pieces.

—*Soledad Perez Bernal*, crab picker

Mexican crab pickers trained by Laurena Collemer. *Photo: Kelly Feltault.*

It was a long, long bus trip to get here. We left Monterrey at 1:00 p.m. on Monday and arrived here on Wednesday at 2:00 p.m. It was a direct bus from Laredo, Texas; two days in the bus, night and day. The bus only stops if we have to change buses and when we stop to eat.

We get all our tickets from Monterrey to El Paso. In El Paso the bus stops on the Mexican side and we have to cross the bridge to the other side by foot. It is right there, at the other side of the bridge, where we get our passports and working permits. We pay for the bus fare and everything else ourselves. This year we paid $105.00 from Monterrey to the Island.

—*Guadelupe Garcia Ortiz*, crab picker

In two days' time, I had them all picking crabs. But I worked with 'em. Then I had them picking in their can because they wanted to pick it in their pan, pile the meat all up, and then they would take time picking over it and getting the bones out of it and everything. And we can't do that, you have to pick right into the can according to the law.

—*Laurena Collemer*, local crab picker

It did not take me too long to learn. We arrived on a Wednesday and on Thursday they took us to the plant to observe, not only to watch but they let us try our own way. You learn a lot by watching others. Now we teach the new girls.

—*Graciela Ponte*, crab picker

Even the Americans will tell you they've just never seen anybody pick it up so fast. Rosetta, she's been picking crabs, I don't know, forty or fifty years, she's seventy-five years old now. And when she was here, the girls were learning, and she would watch 'em, and she was beating 'em bad. Then it got to the point they were gaining on her. Then next year they'd come back, they'd caught her. And then the next year, they passed her.

—*Jay Newcomb*, manager,
  A. E. Phillips Seafood

Our contract says we are supposed to pick twenty-two pounds and three-quarters after three weeks of training. If we cannot reach that goal, we are sent back to Mexico. After we reach that goal, we start getting paid per pound we produce, before that we were paid by the hour. Now, working until 2 p.m. we make about twenty-three or twenty-four pounds, but it all depends on how fleshy the crabs are. Today they were not good.

—*Aracely Hernandez Salinas,* crab picker

The Mexican pickers pay their own rent. They cannot pay rent if it puts 'em below minimum wage, but you can for a domestic worker. I mean a U.S. worker, if they only make $5.15 an hour times 40 hours, two hundred and some dollars, they can still pay rent. But when a migrant worker comes in here and only makes that, they don't have to pay rent. So we rephrased it now that they pay rent per season so that offsets it instead of per week 'cause one week you make a lot of overtime, so we just left it as per season for the rent.

—*Jay Newcomb,* manager,
  A. E. Phillips Seafood

We pay $25.00 per week in rent everything included. But we asked for Spanish cable TV which we pay extra for, and we also asked for a telephone upstairs for which we each pay $2.00 extra per month.

—*Soledad Perez Bernal,* crab picker

Don Tono comes here on weekends from Easton with his van full of Mexican merchandise. We buy chocolate from Morelia, tortillas, cheese, peppers—ingredients to make tacos. Another lady in the house gets up earlier on the weekends in order to cook, sometimes she starts the night before. Sometimes we eat crabmeat, we heat it with tomatoes, cilantro, and onion. But we miss the food, the music of home and feel very isolated here.

We spend the feast of the Immaculate Conception here and many big Mexican festivities here—November 20th, and our Independence Day on September 16th. We celebrate by sleeping all the time and try not to think of how they are celebrating at home. Although we are thinking, just thinking, how nice it would be if we could get together with the Mexican girls from the other plants and have a big celebration, but we are just thinking about it. Last year we celebrated among ourselves and nobody understood why or what were we celebrating because nobody here knows anything about Mexico.

—*Aracely Hernandez Salinas,* crab picker

Sometimes we are able to go to church. I don't think there is a Catholic church here, but we go to Phillips Seafood where Father Joel has services every week in the picking room.

—*Lily Alarcon,* crab picker

My children are too small to understand. One is three years old and the other one is nine months of age, but some day I will tell them that I had to go very far away to work, that I made the sacrifice of leaving them behind. I hope that my children will not have to make the sacrifice I had to make and that they will have better jobs.

—*Vincenta Garcia Ortiz,* crab picker

I tell lies. I tell my parents that it is easy work, that it is not too tiring. But last year when I came home my father took my hands into his, looked at them and said, "You have worked hard."

—*Lily Alarcon,* crab picker

Bishop Joel Johnson leads services in the picking room of A. E. Phillips Seafood. *Photo: Kelly Feltault.*

When we leave here we leave crying. We leave memories and have to separate from each other in our houses after having been so close for such a long time. But once we cross the border into Mexico our feelings change. All our thoughts are about the home of our parents. Actually I like it; it is a way of life. When I go home I am happy that I am going to see my family and old friends again. When I come back here I am looking forward to seeing my old co-workers again, and I know that after a few long months I will be going back home again.

—*Maria Cuevas Hernandez,* crab picker

Long before Mexican crab pickers arrived, women had picked crabmeat illegally in their homes. They sold it to local restaurants, family, and friends in spite of health department regulations. Many women felt this was the only way to raise small children and still work.

In the 1990s, Maryland forced the "bootleg pickers" of Smith Island—and many others—to "go legal" at the urging of the Chesapeake Seafood Packer's Association. Women, who had picked for years in their homes, now built mini plants and employed family members. However, the women of Tylerton, led by Janice Marshall, banded together and formed the Smith Island Crab Meat Co-Operative, a factory unlike any other on the Chesapeake Bay.

On your trip here you might realize how isolated Smith Island is. So it would figure that if women want to work, it's not too many career options. So, if you don't want to work in seafood, you're sunk. Over the years, women have found out that picking crabs helped provide a little extra money for the family. That's how it started—two or three wives started picking their husbands crabs and selling the meat themselves, well by word of mouth, everybody says well I think I can do it.

Crabmeat had been confiscated off the depot in Crisfield, off the island ferry, two or three times that year. And it hadn't been my crabmeat, but I was just holding my breath. And one day, low and behold, I get on the ferry with my box of crabmeat and go on to Crisfield, and there they are waiting—Health Department and Department of Natural Resources. And make a long story short; they got me that day. But the day mine was took, it come to me; this is what you've come to depend on, this is why you're able to live and stay on Smith Island. This is coming to an end right here today and now because they've got you.

They just took the crabmeat out of the truck, and I asked for a search warrant. They said they didn't need one. But we had a slight confrontation on the depot—I threatened to throw the health department man overboard. I asked the DNR policeman, I said, "If I accidentally bump this man and knock him overboard, can you arrest me?" He said, "Well if it was an accident." I said, "It's an accident, here he goes." But he moved just in time. But you know, when your way of life is threatened, you fight back. So the fight got in me, I guess. And that's when we started the coop.

—*Janice Marshall,* crab picker, Smith Island Crab Meat Co-Operative

Booming Blackmarket in Crabmeat Reported Here

—*The Banner,* June 15, 1977.

I can remember when my mother and father had a restaurant and a grocery store in Crisfield—this is probably 35 years ago—when the state inspectors would get a hold of home picked meat they would pour bleach on it. I can remember we'd buy a lot of frozen crabmeat for our restaurant. And when mom would hear that they're coming around checking, we'd have to go get boxfuls of crabmeat and take it to other people's freezers or to other friends' houses and get it out of the store because it was illegal.

—*Patty Laird,* crab picker,
Smith Island Crabmeat Co-operative

I'll tell you something else, as far as bootlegging, I'm not as brave as some of the other women around here. I'd rather stay on the good side of the law. And I just thought, you know, why not try this coop; let's go into it. Suppose they should put a halt on us picking all together. I mean it's possible. And I thought I've just got to have some income coming in. We're no different than the ones on the mainland; takes two to make a living.

—*Christine Smith,* crab picker, Smith Island Crab Meat Co-Operative

Really, it's like fifteen independent businesses under one roof. You have no boss here to work for. We know what's expected of us from the health department and everybody goes about their job and does it. We have a board of directors and a president that takes care of running the building.

You can't dump everybody's crabs in a big basket to steam them like on the mainland. You've got to know which crabs are yours, so when your husband brings them in, we steam 'em in the basket, put our name on it. That way, everybody gets to pick their husband's crabs. You get to sell to your own customers. Very simple. At the end of the week, they tally up how many pounds they've picked, and for every pound of crabmeat I pick, I pay $2.00 to the co-op. So if I pick 100 pound one week, the co-op gets $200.00 of my money. That's how we run the business.

—*Janice Marshall,* crab picker, Smith Island Crab Meat Co-Operative

How did I have to do it? It wasn't easy. It took a lot of time. My sister had put her own mini plant in, so I went by her telling me. But the lady from the Health Department helped me an awful lot to make sure everything was right. I think it took me the most parts of two years. You had to get the septic system in and apply for all of the permits. And today, it's working nice. I have the steamer, the crate, the cooler, and the picking room. And I use my home for the toilet. My husband had retired. I think it took about $40,000.00 to build. We spent most of his retirement. Then he died two years later, which made it very hard on me.

—*Betty Lou Middleton,* champion crab picker, owner, Fast Fingers Seafood

The Smith Island Crab Meat Co-Operative is one of a handful of new mini-plants. *Photo: Kelly Feltault.*

I've had a problem with the mini plants ever since they started because it was a stepping stone for 'em to get into the business. Once they got started picking the crabs, then they grew, and they're up to a full-grown plant now. When the state started this they had to be less than five pickers, and they had to be all family. They did not have to have a bathroom. They could go in their house and use the bathroom. It was all family; the men were watermen and the wives picked the crabs. And now they're all foreign labor with over 25 pickers. The health department went along with this mini plant law because it would stop some from picking in the back yard, picking black market crabmeat.

—*Jay Newcomb,* manager,
  A. E. Phillips Seafood

SHORTAGE: CRABS

Before the 1940s, crab picking houses picked 95% of all the crabs they bought and only 5% of the crabs were shipped live for steamed crabs. People did not order a bushel of crabs to steam at home on the fourth of July, so everything went to the pickers regardless of size. Crabs are culled according to size today, and large crabs are shipped to the "City Market" in what locals call the "basket trade." This leaves crab pickers with only the smaller crabs to pick. Some packers site the consumer demand for crab feasts as one of the factors contributing to the crab shortage.

Crab catches have always fluctuated, but the first time the industry felt any significant impact of an impending crab shortage occurred in 1968. Crabs were so scarce that year that many of the Bay's smaller packers went out of business, and the federal government held a congressional hearing on the issue. Today, the majority of crabs picked in Maryland are caught in North Carolina and trucked to the waiting crab houses.

You got up in the morning, you were going to Tilghman Packing Company to work. You were coming home from Tilghman Packing in the afternoon, going back the next day. And all that suddenly stopped completely. It was quite a shock when they closed. I think everybody felt the same way probably that I did. What are we going to do now?

—*Lib Dunleavy,* crab picker

If all the conditions is pretty good, then I know I can leave in a certain time and make $100.00. That means you have to be motivated for one thing. And then the crabs you're working on have to be good. They have to be large. But I'm a claw cracker, so if the claws are small, that means I have to crack too many of 'em to get anything. Like years ago when they were so large—this is the truth— that you could take about seventeen, eighteen claws and get a pound of meat. That means I cracked them seventeen, eighteen claws in a minute and a half, and you could take about five claws, get over a quarter pound of meat, or maybe a third of a pound. And them days are gone.

—*Donald Cephas,* claw cracker

Most the time here, our local crabbers are in by 3:00 in the afternoon. But we have a truck in North Carolina because it's not enough crabs here. Not enough to work full time. So we're down there three or four times a week.

—*W. T. Ruark,* owner, W. T. Ruark Seafood

Jay Newcomb unloads crabs from North Carolina. *Photo: Kelly Feltault.*

Not only do today's crab houses work within a global economy for labor, but they also compete with foreign crabmeat produced in Asia and South America. Consumer demand for crabmeat far exceeds supplies of the local resource and continues outside of crab season. Asian crabmeat has always been part of the American market, but in 1997, as a response to demand, the import levels sharply increased. Asian crabmeat now holds 70% of that market.

Packing house owners emphatically state the real problem is confusion over labeling. Do consumers know they are buying *Portunis pelagicus* from Asia rather than the local *Callinectes sapidus*—blue swimming crab versus blue crab? Today imported crabmeat is one of the most contested topics in the industry and among Maryland legislators. Solutions are complicated by the fact that domestic companies now own crab factories in Asia.

Everybody will tell you the amount of domestic meat has been declining year after year. Four years ago Phillips Seafood restaurants had put a surcharge on all their menus for crabmeat because it was so high. There's just not enough crabmeat to go around and the price goes up.

—Jay Newcomb, manager,
  A. E. Phillips Seafood

We've seen crabs decline for the last seven, eight, ten years. One reason is the rockfish; you've seen a big difference since these rockfish come back into the Bay. But the biggest issue we got, and it's going to be a serious one 'cause if something don't happen probably two years from now, it won't be no more crab house—I'm talking about imported crabmeat, foreign crabmeat. Fifty cents a day labor over there in China or Asia. You can buy Chinese jumbo lump $5.00 something a pound, ours is $16.00. We can't compete—no way possible.

—W. T. Ruark, owner, W. T. Ruark and Company

Logo for crabmeat picked locally. *Photo: Maryland Department of Agriculture, Seafood Marketing Office.*

"'There were plenty of *[Portunis]* crabs in the Philippines, but no real industry,' Steve says. 'So I went to Asia, took crab pots, and lived with local watermen, figuring out the best ways to catch them.' Phillips Foods today includes an Asian crabmeat empire that employs some 10,000 workers at eight plants in the Philippines, Indonesia and Thailand, with ventures planned in India and Malaysia."

—Steve Phillips, *Chesapeake Magazine*, July 2000.

"Those Phillips 'Maryland style' crab cakes in the grocery's frozen food section—one of the seafood industry's hottest products—are made in Baltimore, but the crabmeat mostly comes from Indonesia, Thailand or the Philippines.

While none of the Asian crabmeat comes from the Atlantic blue crab its marketers often label it 'blue crab.' The practice is legal."

—*The Baltimore Sun*, June 27, 1999.

This bill would require the same kind of labeling that is current law for raw crabmeat, that is, a marking 'displayed in letters not smaller than 12-point type of the principal display panel of the container so as to be easily read by the consumer', and to read 'this product contains crabmeat from (name of country of origin).'

—Delegate Richard D'Amato,
Testimony supporting HB 69—Imported crabmeat restrictions,
February 8, 2000.

Crabmeat legislation shot down

—*The Capital*, Saturday March 4, 2000.

The U. S. Food and Drug Administration is currently looking at other labeling laws proposed by the industry, and the state of Maryland will consider additional crab harvesting regulations in 2001. Regardless of the causes for the decline in the local industry, the Chesapeake Bay may have to find another icon of summer as more and more crab packing plants close each year. However, crab pickers like Laurena Collemer, and the others in this booklet, will continue to work as long as there are crabs.

> Crab pickers never retire. They pick 'til they die there or they come home and die. But you don't retire. It's just something you like to do. My sister is eighty-four, and she's still picking crabs—we just like to do it. It's better than sitting here at home all the time. You could dust and clean every day if you wanted to, but then that wears the carpet out and wears the furniture to pieces, and we weren't brought up to be lazy.

—*Laurena Collemer,* local crab picker

PROFILES

Lily Alarcon is from Hidalgo Mexico, and picks crabs at Rippons Brothers' Seafood in Hoopersville. She has picked crabs for three years.

Soledad Perez Bernal comes from Mayari in Mexico. She works at A. E. Phillips Seafood and has picked crabs for five years.

J. Clayton Brooks has kept J. M. Clayton Company in the family for three generations. Begun in 1890, it is the oldest working crab house on the Eastern Shore.

Rosalie Brown works at J. M. Clayton Company where her mother, Fronie Jones, worked for over eighty years.

Donald Cephas works at J. M. Clayton Company, and is the fastest claw cracker on the Eastern Shore.

Georgia Cephas works at J. M. Clayton Company, and is a descendant of Fronie Jones.

Laurena Collemer works at J. M. Clayton Company. Originally from Hooper's Island, she has picked crabs for over forty-five years. She now trains the Mexican pickers.

Jim Dodson owns and manages Byrd's Seafood and a restaurant in Crisfield.

Lib Dunleavy worked at Tilghman Packing Company until it closed. She is the namesake of *Miss Lib's Crab Cakes* produced by the company.

Joyce Fitchett is an eight time crab picking champion. She has worked at Byrd's Seafood and Maryland Crab Meat Company in Crisfield and now works for the Eastern Shore Correctional Institute.

Nellie Flowers works at W. T. Ruark and Company with her sister. She has picked crabs here for over forty years

Roy Harrison managed Harrison and Jarboe Seafood until he retired and the company was sold. The original factory stood on the site of the Chesapeake Bay Maritime Museum.

Maria Cuevas Hernandez works at Rippons Brothers Seafood in Hoopersville and is from Hidalgo, Mexico. She has picked crabs for three years.

Tim Howard grew up working in the Maryland Crab Meat Company, running it until the company closed in 1999.

Nicie Jones works at J. M. Clayton Company with other members of her family. She has picked crabs here for over fifty years.

Joyce Jones works at J. M. Clayton Company with other members of her family.

Patty Laird lives on Smith Island. She was one of the founders of the Smith Island Crab Meat Co-Operative.

Janice Marshall was one of the founders of the Smith Island Crab Meat Co-Operative, and now works for the Eastern Shore Correctional Institute.

Betty Lou Middleton holds the record for most crabmeat picked at the Crisfield Crab Picking Derby. She won seven times, and retired last year.

Jay Newcomb manages A.E. Phillips Seafood in Fishing Creek. He was the first manager to bring in Mexican pickers.

Alice Palmer continues to crack claws for Higgins Crab House. She still lives in the St. Michaels area and is active in the Methodist Women's Association.

Orlando Purnell was the last president of Local 453, and works with community members to tell the story of the union.

Guadelupe Garcia Ortiz works at W. T. Ruark. She comes from Michoacan and has picked crabs for four years.

Vincenta Garcia Ortiz works at W. T. Ruark with her sister, Guadelupe. She has picked crabs for four years.

Evelyn Robinson works at Meredith and Meredith Inc., and writes editorials on crab picking and the seafood industry. She has picked crabs for over forty-five years.

Aracely Hernandez Salinas is from San Luis Potosi in Mexico and works at Rippons Brothers' Seafood in Hoopersville. She has picked crabs for three years.

Christine Smith is a member of the Smith Island Crab Meat Co-Operative.

I.T. Todd runs Metompkin Seafood with his son. They are one of the few packing houses still open in Crisfield, and one of the oldest.

Calvert Tolley passed on Meredith and Meredith Inc., and Toddville Seafood to his sons. He was one of the creators of the Quik Pik picking machine.

Nicey Turpin was the shop steward for Maryland Crab Meat Company and continued to pick crabs there until that company closed.

ACKNOWLEDGEMENTS

In 1998 The Breene M. Kerr Center for Chesapeake Studies at the Chesapeake Bay Maritime Museum asked me to conduct oral histories and folklife documentation with Eastern Shore crab pickers and packing house owners. I recorded over fifty oral histories, and searched archives for industry records. Many of the pickers and packing house owners gave generously of their time, knowledge and family collections. I want to thank all of the women and men that I interviewed for sharing their experiences and for teaching me the "proper way to pick a crab." I would also like to thank the National Endowment for the Humanities, the Maryland Historical Trust's Cultural Conservation Program, the Grayce B. Kerr Fund, the Maryland Humanities Council, the William H. Combs Jr. Publication Fund, and the Kerr Center for Chesapeake Studies for their support of this project. The mission of the Kerr Center for Chesapeake Studies is to conduct and promote regional humanities research, education, and outreach focused on the interrelationships of nature and culture in the Chesapeake region. There is no stronger connection between culture and environment here than that of the blue crab.

This project was made possible by:

Maryland Historical Trust

Grayce B. Kerr Fund

Maryland Humanities Council through a grant from the National Endowment for the Humanities

William H. Combs Jr. Publication Fund